Now We Wait

Poetry about the Perry High School shooting

Written by

JMR

Copyright © 2024 by Jason Michael Rogers. All Rights reserved. Published independently in the United States.

Cover photo by lxxxm379

First edition. Trade paperback.

ISBN: 9798883511133

Intro

What the hell? A school shooting right as the new year rolls around? Bullying continues to run rampant in the school systems, and teachers – more often than not – are overworked or have their hands tied. They want to get home and rest or they are severely limited in what they can do in terms of advocating for certain students. As a lifelong teacher, I am aware of the burnout and the stress forced down from the School Board.

I've been part of the numerous active shooter trainings and drills.

I've seen stricter rules about backpacks, additional metal detectors, more resource officers, etc. And, I've seen school shootings continue despite stricter gun laws.

Personally, I think the solution is clear, but I know that School Boards detest logic and run from reasonable solutions.

I will keep trying, though. I love teaching and I do it for the students.

In memory of the victims of the shooting in Perry, Iowa.

Now We Wait

He Is Number Four

Perry High School

Is the fourth –

On 1/4 even –

Mass Shooting

In 2024

People,

Gun advocates,

Liberals,

Talking heads,

and whoever

Will jump up

And shout shout

Until some

Now We Wait

Pop star

Hits the news

And says we need

To destroy the

Constitution –

Rip it up like a

Discarded 49ers'

Jersey

Now We Wait

Thoughts & Prayers

I'm sending

Tennis rackets & Condoms,

Bricks & Half a pack of baby wipes,

A VHS copy of *Speed* & Llamas,

Moldy peanut butter & an AA battery,

A postcard from Stonehenge & a Bullet,

Thoughts & Prayers,

And Facebook likes & Tiktok hits...

I'm sending

All things useless

To the victims of Perry High School

Now We Wait

Further Activism

We need to...
Did you see all the
Footage of Taylor Swift
At SuperBowl LVlll?
I can't believe she got
So much footage
She's just dating Kelce
What the hell?
What's Perry again?
Isn't he a Kansas City player?
No, that's Ed Perry – former player.
Ed Perry played as a tight end
For the Kansas City Chiefs

Now We Wait

He was primarily known
for his time with
The Miami Dolphins,
where he spent the
Majority of his career.
Perry was drafted
By the Dolphins in the
6th round of the 2000 NFL
Draft and played
For Miami until 2005.
After his stint with the
Dolphins, he had
Short tenures with the
Chiefs and the
Denver Broncos.
Perry was recognized

Now We Wait

for his blocking ability

And contributed

to the teams he played

for during his NFL career

Wait...

What were we talking about?

Ah, who's gonna go

All the way next season?

Now We Wait

A School Shooting

happened again – yet again –
So we need to give our
Guns to the government
We don't trust in the first place
Instead of solving the actual problem
That causes school shootings
Guns are the weapons
Bullying is the cause
(One of them)

Now We Wait

One More Time

for those in the back

It's bullying.

Bullying's the cause.

For readers and reviewers

And random viewers,

It's bullying.

Bullying's the cause.

I'll say it again

Spout it and yell

Now We Wait

Popularity

Everyone will remember

Dylan Butler

We expect a Netflix

Making of a Murderer about

Dylan Butler

We expect news report

After news report about

Dylan Butler

We look forward to a

Film about Dylan Butler

But we will never

Now We Wait

Hear the name of a

Victim

Now We Wait

Could You Bring

some attention on
this, David Hogg?

Now We Wait

Was It Just Me

or.... could anyone else
Not find a date to the
Prom? Was it the End?
The end of the world?
Apocalypses lined up
Like students in
The lunch room?
I cried and leveled up
My angst, but I
Happily graduated and
Flipped off that
Hellhole of a school
Never to return again

Now We Wait

Hell, I couldn't see it

From the brightness

Of my future ahead

Fuck those bullies

Back then

Fuck all them ops

I don't even remember

All their venial names

Now We Wait

Was It Also You

who got bullied and

Bullied and bullied

as the teacher's

Waved it off like

A crumb on their

Shoulder?

Their brush off

Was the internal

Painful slap

Now We Wait

Solution

He was bullied

So we need to give up

Our guns

He knows he will

Be popular –

Netflix special as part

Of their Serial Killer Universe

So we need to give up

Our guns

We need more social

Workers and therapists

In schools

Or, we need to give up

Now We Wait

Our guns

He listened to KMFDM,

Which was a favorite song

Of Eric Harris (Columbine)

So we need to give up

Our guns

Now We Wait

The 80's

We had guns

All through the 80's

When I was young

But there were no

School shootings

But, it must be a

Gun problem

Gun laws – every

year – become

tighter and stricter

but there are more

School shootings

Now We Wait

Poor

Poor NRA

You get blamed

For a school

Shooting

When the

Problem

Stares everyone

In their

Apathetic and

ACME faces

Now We Wait

But, Me?

Senator Chuck Grassely released
A statement:

Look at me. Don't forget about me. I know today was bad, but I need the spotlight.

Now We Wait

Wording

It's only been
Two days or so
And I'm waiting
For "assault weapon"
To pop its ugly head
Up again
Is the Ukraine
Still at war?
Didn't Israel have
Some issues with
Another country?
How's my crypto?
I need to check.

Now We Wait

Distracted wreck

Of a person I am,

Playing Solitaire too much

Now We Wait

Guns

is all we want to

Hear about now

Nothing about bullying

Or lack of access

To mental help or

Wanting to be famous

No no no no no

GUNS GUNS GUNS

Take those away

Then we can watch

Bullied kids and

Kids in need of

Mental health help

Now We Wait

And kids who want to
Be famous use IED's,
Bombs, and knives to
Cause havoc in schools
Just as long as we can
Talk about the Guns
Fuck the realities of
Bullying – especially
Cyber-bullying
Fuck the need to catch
The antecedents which
Will Help kids and
Fuck the fact that kids
Look up to the Joker
And Dexter and Thanos,
And love shows about Bundy

Now We Wait

And Dahmer and Gacy,

Thinking, "Hey, I can be

Famous, too."

Fuck all that and let me give

You my two cents – but only

Towards gun control groups

Because my thoughts are taken

With a focus on the wrong thing

This is not me January 4th, 2024

This has been me since Pearl, Ms

And Columbine

Our societal attention

Is fleeting – tweaker leaping

From one distraction to

Another – what should I

Care about tomorrow?

Now We Wait

My slacktivism is aching

Now We Wait

Stricter Gun Laws

are made – tighter and tighter

with loop holes sealed

Every school shooting

brings useless legislation

Millions spent on

Bridges to nowhere

As nine school shootings

Echo out the first

Fifty-seven days of this

Depressing year

I could say important

Points twice and three times

Like I have but apathy will

Now We Wait

Block the lessons

Now We Wait

Armed Teachers

Teachers should not be
Armed – I say as a
Lifelong teacher
Having a permit – a
Conceal and carry is
One thing, but
Threat assessment is
Another beast
Just wait for a chaotic,
Stressful situation
Kids crying and scared
And running from hell
Just wait for that one

Now We Wait

White teacher to shoot

That one black kid

And everyone will

Lose their minds

Until the next 'thing'

Comes around

Now We Wait

RIP

RIP Ahmir Joliff

Now We Wait

Irony

Many who shout

And graffiti ACAB

Are the ones who

Want only the

Police to be armed

After...

A school shooting

Happens.

Now We Wait

Gun Laws

change

And someone shoots

Up a School

Gun Laws

Change

And someone shoots

Up a School

Gun Laws

Change

And someone shoots

Up a School

Gun Laws

Change

Now We Wait

And someone shoots

Up a School

Gun Laws

Change

And someone shoots

Up a School

Gun Laws

Change

And.... ∞

Now We Wait

Laws

are made to

Classify

'assault weapons'

And lawyers are

Brought in to

Find loopholes

They always do

New weapon made –

Very similar –

But it's not an

assault weapon

According to the law

Now We Wait

Tears

flow and grief

Cripples – as

Trauma haunts,

But I write

This poetry,

Hoping people

Will hear my

Words

I am no

better – maybe

Worse than

Anyone else

Now We Wait

He Got

tunnel vision

With bullies in

His sights

And the small

Barrel pointed

Back at himself

In the End

Now We Wait

But, There Is

no end

Now We Wait

There Isn't

even a middle

Not this year

Now We Wait

Dylan

Didn't
Break any
Gun laws

Now We Wait

RIP

RIP Ahmir Joliff

Remember

Because we

Missed the eulogies

At St. Patrick

Catholic Church

Now We Wait

RIP

RIP Ahmir Joliff

Remember

Always

Not the shooter

Remember the

Victims and

Honor them

Now We Wait

Hero

Dan Marburger

Is a hero

Teachers are

Uncared for

Heroes by name only

Now We Wait

RIP

Marburger
This is an
Update

Now We Wait

RIP

Any future

normality

In Perry

Now We Wait

Dylan's

sister was

Also being bullied

Have you

ever had a

Loved one

begin your

Torment right

In front of you?

Now We Wait

The Problem

~~are guns~~

is the educational system

And the sideways

Glances the wrong way

A smile at the bullies

And a "Oh, it wasn't

that bad" to the

Bullied

Now We Wait

The Police

found a pump action rifle

And a small caliber pistol

CHANGE ALL GUN LAWS!

Now We Wait

7:37 am

saw the first alert

7:44 am

saw the first responders

Seven minutes

less time than

Chauvin had his

Knee on Floyd's

Neck

Now We Wait

Maybe

Will you listen now with this format?

Now We Wait

Emulating

the Cook from

Texas Chainsaw Massacre

And Jeffrey Dahmer

But Guns are the problem

Eric and Dylan have

Been often emulated

Now We Wait

Sad

"Question for those who haven't started transitioning yet. What's holding you back?"

"I don't want to look ugly."

⬆ are the only social media ⬆
⬆ posts of Dylan's I could find ⬆
⬆ They were deleted quickly ⬆
⬆ Was there more to his pain? ⬆

Now We Wait

Damn

Gov. Kim Reynolds
Said flag to be flown
As half-mast
This is the patriotic
thoughts & prayers

Now We Wait

Broken

The educational system is broken

The criminal justice system, too

Politics are, of course, corrupt,

Useless, and a zoo – feral & wild

But I will won't stop being a

Teacher

Now We Wait

The Bell Rings

24th for elementary

25th for middle

Face the trauma

Again

Full time classes

A little later

And the healing

Probably never

Now We Wait

Maybe

Maybe

if there were more therapists

Maybe

if there was easier access to help

Maybe

if bullying was addressed

Maybe

if the school could advocate for those

who are bullied

Maybe

if people weren't bigots

Maybe

If I had a say, but...

I'm just a pen and paper owner

Now We Wait

And an English teacher –

Licensed and experienced

Maybe

If the obvious could jump

And scream louder

Maybe

If Obvious was a celebrity,

He would get a listen

Now We Wait

Thoughts & Prayers

moved on quickly

Thoughts on whatever

And prayers for

Their favorite nothing

Their hated nothing

Your controlled focus

Darts away – to and fro

Now We Wait

House Bill

2586 passed

but the bullies

Still reign

Unpunished

Unchanged

Unconcerned

Their bravado

Barrels towards

Those needing

Advocating – they

Walk unperturbed

Now We Wait

RIP

RIP Ahmir Joliff

Remember

Always

Forget Dylan

Erase Dyla

Delete Dyl

RIP Dan Marburger

Remember

Always

Backspace Dy

Scrub out D

Now, the victims

Remain

Now We Wait

Now We Wait

For nothing to change

Made in the USA
Coppell, TX
09 December 2024